Adventures

The Crystal Planet

Karen Ball • Jonatronix

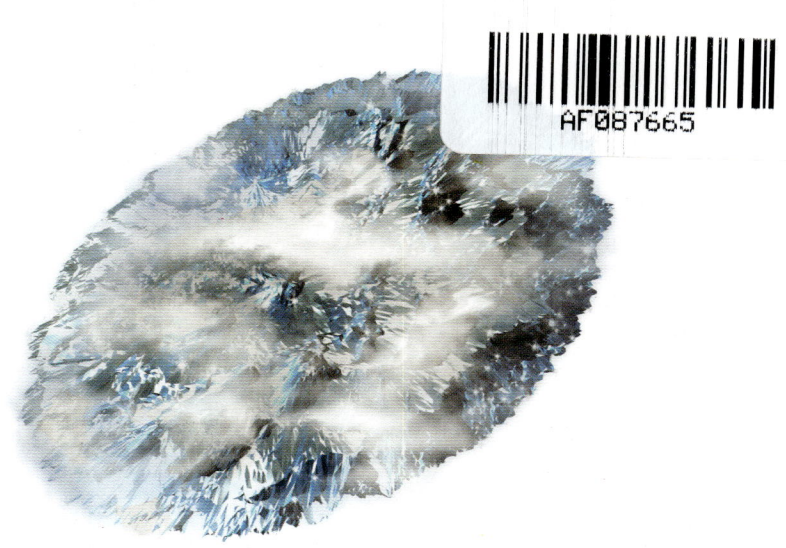

OXFORD
UNIVERSITY PRESS

Max's mission log

We are travelling through space on board the micro-ship Excelsa with our new friends, Nok and Seven.

We're on a mission to save Planet Exis (Nok's home planet), which is running out of power. We need to collect four fragments that have been hidden throughout the Beta-Prime Galaxy. Together the fragments form the Core of Exis. Only the Core will restore power to the planet.

It's not easy. A space villain called Badlaw wants the power of the Core for himself. His army of robotic Krools is never far behind us!

Fragments collected so far: 1

The Beta-Prime Galaxy
Destination: Planet Celeston

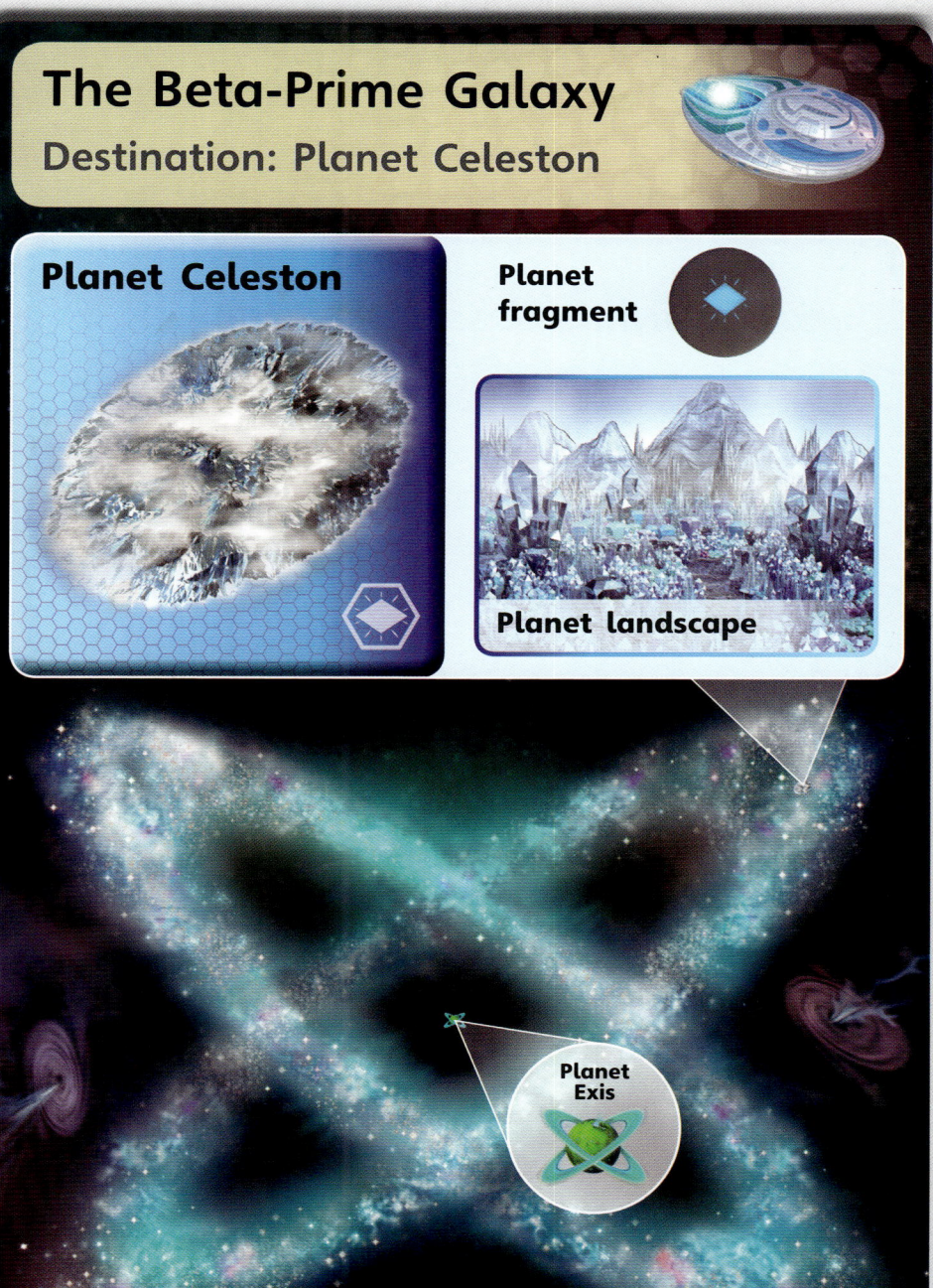

Planet Celeston

Planet fragment

Planet landscape

Planet Exis

Chapter 1 – Crash-landing

The ship began to shudder. Cat ran to her station.

"*Impact warning!*" said the ship.

"We're in Celeston's gravity field," said Ant, looking helplessly at the panel in front of him. "It's dragging us down."

"Can you slow the ship, Nok?" asked Max.

Nok pulled back on the steering orbs. "The gravity is too strong!" he shouted.

They were still dropping fast.

"We are going to crash!" cried Seven.

The ship broke through a layer of thick cloud. It plunged down towards the surface of the planet.

"Whoa!" gasped Tiger, as he saw the glittering rocks below.

"Hold on!" Nok yelled. "It's going to be a rough landing."

The ship thudded along the ground. Nok did his best to steer between the huge crystals.

Finally, they came to a juddery halt.

Planet Celeston

Information

Planet Celeston is one of the brightest planets in the Beta-Prime Galaxy. It is known as the 'diamond planet' because of its sparkling, diamond-like appearance.

Known life forms
- Minatrolls
- Pyrite Panthers

Surface conditions
- Strong gravity
- Frequent mineral storms
- Rocky terrain

- **disc-shaped**
- **mineral clouds**
- **glittering surface**
- **rocky terrain**

Chapter 2 – First steps

"Ant, we need a damage report," Max ordered.

"I'm running one now," said Ant. "Some of the rear power cells are broken," he replied, a moment later.

"We can't take off without them," said Tiger.

"Come on. Let's see how bad it is," said Max.

As soon as Max stepped off the ship, his whole body felt heavy.

Tiger slumped down next to him. "My arms and legs feel like concrete," he groaned.

"You need to adjust your suits to adapt to the planet's gravity," Seven called from the exit hatch.

Chapter 3 – On with the mission

Max and Tiger adjusted their suits. Then they made their way to the back of the ship to assess the damage. Seven was hovering beside them.

Tiger pointed to a large crack running along the power cells. "That's our problem," he said.

Seven opened the hatch in his stomach. He took out a tube.

"I can fix it," he said.

"How?" asked Max.

"This is a special gel that will seal the crack," replied Seven. "But it will need time to dry."

Cat, Ant and Nok joined them at the rear of the ship.

"Ant, can you stay here with Tiger and Seven and finish fixing the ship?" Max asked. "I'll go with Cat and Nok to look for the fragment."

"No problem," said Ant.

Nok was staring hard into the distance. "I think we need to go that way," he said.

"How do you know?" asked Cat.

"I can feel the energy from the fragment," Nok replied. "It's pulling me towards it."

"Let's get going then," said Max.

Max, Cat and Nok pressed their buttons. They all grew to normal size.

The three of them set off.

Chapter 4 – Mineral storm

Max, Cat and Nok followed a long, rocky path.

Cat flipped up the magni-scope on her watch.

"There is a cave up ahead," she said. "Maybe the fragment will be in there."

The cave was further away than they expected. Max felt like he had been walking forever.

"Come on!" Nok said, walking past him. He was desperate to find the next fragment.

Just then, a glistening cloud of dust blew around them.

"It's a mineral storm!" cried Nok, breaking into a run. "Quick, we need to get to the cave!"

The shimmering dust began to swirl faster. They started to cough and splutter.

Chapter 5 – The map

At last, they found the entrance to the cave. Max, Cat and Nok ran inside and leant against a wall to catch their breath.

The cave sparkled. It looked as if the walls were covered in tiny stars.

"Wow," said Cat, gazing round.

"Where's the fragment?" asked Max.

Nok spotted a picture etched into the wall. As he touched it, blue power surged from his hand, lighting it up.

"It wasn't the energy from the fragment I could feel after all," he said. "It was this."

"It's a map," said Cat.

"My people must have drawn it when they left the fragment," said Nok.

"Look, there's an X," Max said. He pointed to an etching of a pyramid. "That must be where the fragment is hidden."

They walked to the mouth of the cave. The storm was disappearing over the horizon.

"Let's go," said Max. "We'll just have to hope that the others can catch up …"

Max's voice was drowned out by a growling noise coming from inside the cave.

Max looked over his shoulder. Two pairs of glittering eyes looked back at him.

"I think we've got company," he said, his voice trembling.

Find out what happens next in *The Ruby Cage*.